ANOTHER BREATH

ANOTHER BREATH

Josie Walsh

Ox-Eye Press
2009

Published 2009
Ox Eye Press
79 Oxford Street
OX20 1TJ

Cover Design: Pen2print

ISBN:978-1-50446-58-9

ACKNOWLEDGEMENTS

Thanks are due to the editors of the following magazines
or anthologies: *Aireings, Cathedral News, Cracking On,
Forty Years of Pennine Poets: Mind and Body,
Forty Years of Pennine Poets: Spirit and Emotion,
Friendly Street (Aus), Front Runner, Full Gallop,
Horse's Mouth, Hope Street, Pennine Platform
and Triangle.*
Thanks are also due to the staff at Wakefield Cathedral and
Pugneys Country Park, particularly Steve Cerrone, Manager
of the park, for his invitation to set up Pugneys *Under Glass,*
believed to be the first poetry magazine of its kind.

*For my family
And everyone with whom I have shared poetry*

CONTENTS

LIMEN

ON DEEP STREET

AS WELL AS SAINTS

ANOTHER BREATH

LIMEN

You can find poetry in your everyday life,
your memory, in what people say on the bus,
in the news, or just what's in your heart.

Carol Ann Duffy, Poet Laureate

LIMEN

I like that word threshold, *limen*
where lie beginnings, borders,
a curious place
where anything might happen.
Where a dawn might break.

No stranger to sudden sunrise
where bamboo creaks and humidity
makes skin a wet swimsuit. I've slept
where *fortissimo* toads deafen snakes.
And the rain forest sweats, a foot away.

Where orioles call, to parrots in neon flightpaths
over the mangroves. And those trees
that have spanned hundreds of summers.
I've crossed high rope-bridges, shaking
over black-mirror water. Breathed delicate air

where prayer-bells echo from ethereal temples.
I've camped on a desert night, so clear
warmongers traded espionage.
Seen a river of people on scooters,
a pillion mother, feeding two babies.

This threshold widens to a light-filled room,
books, plants, pictures.
Here, in the untravelled breath
of the still-sleeping house,
I cross from night to another day.

HOMECOMING

Bright light, harsh, newly arrived.
Skin on the black bone of night.
Sky beginning blue.
Flying earlier than swallows
clocks tick awry, house roots move.
Cold bites through bedding.

The wood pigeon, again,
has colonized the chimney.
Practises its chilling coo.
Through a curtain chink
what seemed snow
is massed magnolia.

It should be midday: savage sun
sweeping the veranda, fans whirring.
The pool, waiting for shade enough to swim.
The baby, waking from a nap, dewy-skinned.
The still air filled with cinnamon
and the starchiness of steaming rice.

Body and heart are dislocated, flown out.
They say eight hours and as many days
to catch up time.
Through the window of myself,
memories open one from another,
babushka dolls in a diminishing line.
Here, a few remaining snowdrops
almost white, droop their heads.
A thrush reclaims the lawn.

ANOTHER WINTER

First frost, I nose out to the hard-surfaced air.
The bird bath, glass-lidded now, has trapped debris,
a red curled leaf, two twigs like wishbones.
Yesterday's prints still show on the shaded path.
Inside on the kitchen window sill, the gift
of home-made marmalade, fine-chopped peel.
Lemon and not too sweet, you said
as coffee spluttered in the metal pot.

This winter measures more than thirty winters here.
Remember that huge icicle above the door?
It merited black-and-white photography,
frost sculpture, fluted forms and edges.
We let it melt, like winter softening to Spring
as ground moved quietly to green climaxing.

PUGNEYS CHRONICLE

January

Short days sail
through the nib's eye.

A double rainbow
arcs over trees, comes to land
among spindle-thin masts,
stilled sailing craft,
making this old mining ground, maritime.

Another New Year.
A child's glove hangs by one finger
on a branch, where a red berry gleams.

February

Rows of gulls on the grass
are like waves blown inland,
by a wind that rips current
through black treacle water.
That makes puddles alive, as if fish
driven frantic, are gasping for air.

Two men chase a dog, its jaws caught
in a red plastic cage.
Sprung limbs are bursting to canter,
its hollowed-out flanks
more at home on a track,
with floodlights and shouting.

March

Purple pastel the hills, blurred
with green trees. The sky, sullen-sulky
as if it would smudge itself out
from a smooth belly of cloud.

Through mud slicks and puddles
crows are cavorting.

Then from the stream, a heron,
all wingspan, a flash
between branches and leaves.
The heron flies as if it is leader.

We turn towards home, to see
two, hind-legged hares, boxing.

April

White clouds move on enamel blue,
in the glassy lake their doubles sail.
Reflected reeds and slender trees
make mirrored, liquid foliage.

This gifted day unfolds in the drowse of heat.

Beyond all this wide shimmering
is the waking, changing skyline.
Crane dinosaurs converse, nod
steel heads, white-latticed, grey.

May

Early May, the white lace is frothing
yards of it cascade along the bank, the lane,
the rows of luminous suburban gardens.

Though wind has blown the prunus and the pear,
chin-high cow parsley effervesces over footpaths.
We shoulder brush its chalky scent, from clusters

filigreed on stems. Everywhere the hawthorn foams.
It swirls and clots from laden branches.
Before its tips tinge pink.

Later, the lipstick reds of peonies, azaleas
will all shout their glory. But for now,
the countryside is creamed and cameoed
against a bank of greens, against a pewter sky.

June

The snails have left a trail
of running stitch, evenly spaced.
The path is zig-zagged
in fluorescent silk.
This is summer.

Water soothes, shines beyond sirens,
police cars, ambulance.
The snails have made hosta leaves
into a cloak of holes.

Whenever the word *silk* comes
it belongs to you:
the red dress cut on the bias,
the embroidered kimono,
the bed jacket, trimmed with swansdown.

A child takes these from padded hangers.
Lays them with care on the bed.
Arranges the skirt till it circles.
Straightens the kimono sleeves.
She nestles the swansdown.

Snails were sewing then.

July

They drift in mist that prefaces the heat,
a dozen one-winged dragonflies.
Transparent sails, they move as magic

until a quiet command
when every surfer, cruciform, takes batons, pinned
across the sail, pulls back, forth, repeatedly.

The beat is huge, much louder
than the swans or geese in winter echelons.
What a conjuror is sound.

Suddenly it is July,
the Orange order, sashed and banging,
menace in the morning air.

August

A month ago
this August field
was thigh-high wheat,
      where the rabbits played
      where the poppies bled.
      Now a posse of crows
      strut the curve of the stubbled slope.
      That stretches like sand, like infinite gold.
      They scare wood-pigeons
      away from the spoils.

And on these nights, a terrible harvest.

      Here are the faces, lit with youth,
      their uniforms trim. They are pasted on screen,
row upon row, like so many stamps.
      Now franked, by Death.

September

Drums, that warning of ancient grievance
or summoning before another war.

Ghostly drums are here.
Foot soldiers, telling with dismay,
the rout, six centuries ago.

Blackberry, brambles, elder and hedge-rose,
the trumpets of convolvulus, summon us
to where the ruined castle, surveys all.

Beneath here they lie, the clean white bones.
How battles, blood, blackberries
and White Rose blur.

October

Ankle-deep amber,
sherbert yellow,
shushes every step.

A young pheasant runs
as if on wheels
below the hovering crow.

A spider at the window pane,
sashays on self-spun thread.
Old wasps crash land.

Sun fools the butterflies.
A sky so lately black
stretches cerulean.

.

November

Even with a week of wind that turns
long grass to fleeing porcupine,
there's still a leafy palette at the Lake.
The wind-flirt birch has dancing ochre.
Berries are magenta.
Willow, one side, has a dab of Chinese white.
The oaks bear a still-rich canopy of leaves,
like fur and gold in a medieval portrait.

Too strong a breeze for the geese,
a feathered flotilla, they moor in the shallow.
Watch the bird men on their surf boards.
Watch the wind whip kayaks.

I like this place, even when sky scowls
and the lake is black.
I love the way on bright days,
light turns the corner on the path.
The way the city's heart, sun-burnished,
rises beyond diamond-dizzy water.

December

Here is the lake,
mud slicks and weed
and watery creatures
that live unobserved.

Here is the lake,
its ducks and coots.
The echeloned geese
beating their wind time.

Here is the Christmas lake,
frost–latticed, empty.
But for the swans
with their Archangel wings.

Pugneys Country Park, previously the site of an open-cast mine, lies below the ruin of Sandal castle. The word 'Pugneys' is Anglo Saxon for Puck or Puca's water meadows. There was a medieval ox-bow lake, known as Pugnals or Pungeys, which means a goblin's nook or a mystical dwelling. In this second *Chronicle*, as in *Breathing Space*, exterior and inner landscape merge. Poems draw on both the actual lake and corresponding lakes of memory, imagination and experience.

GOING TO HOPE STREET *(for J)*

Because you are thousands of miles away
and even further from your childhood,
I cannot see you.
But this morning on the station I heard you.
You were putting something down,
it seemed to have a wheel that was squeaky.

I heard a whirring and it was you drying your hair.
You must have been in a hurry
because normally this is not necessary in the heat.
Maybe you had put that stuff on
to make your hair less curly.
Something fell on a marble floor.
And there was a child's shout, echoing in a stairwell.

Now from the train window, I see a woman
who walks through a bright birch wood.
She is filtered in light, her steps crack the twigs
that lie among ruffs of purple-brown leaves.
The sky is blue agapanthus.

It's the same wood where in Spring,
there are hold-me-tight violets in heart-shaped nests.
I remember you saying
how much you missed frosty mornings.

I needed to rush then on cobbled camber
down shawl and bonnet streets.
But instead of the usual clogs, I heard
I'm absolutely certain I heard, you.
And you were laughing.

HOTMAIL

Summer-high sky defying the winter,
vapour trails cross hatch the blue.
They spring like searchlights
from a sun of blurred gold.
Angle a silver speck plain.

The banks of the lake are melted green
except filigreed ferns, the cobwebbed copse,
where ice lingers, making white coral
out of the grass, starfish
from fallen leaves.

A time zone away your tropical rain,
beating tattoos on the roof.
Splatting on swimming-pool tiles.
Bursting sky canopy.

Here the gulls float in pairs
in glacier water, small craft
waiting to berth.

Not like your dragonflies skimming.
Not like the humming bird, perched
on the banana.

Instead of a letter
I send you this English day, wrapped
in its gifted light, its cold clarity.

LAKE BIRDS
Swallow *(Hirundo rustica)*

Once it was thought, when swallows disappeared,
they'd flown right to the moon, or were hiding
at the bottom of a lake.
With Autumn's breath, they twitter on high wires,
staved like notation in a burst of song.
Then they fly south to the plains of Africa
and winter sun, forerunning package holidays.
They need no factor cream; will not buy paperbacks,
fake Gucci glasses or suffer plane delays.
Will not return sun-scorched or overdrawn,
to tell the neighbours what the hotel was like.
They'll go straight there, feeding as they fly,
pointed wings, streamers on forked tails.

Grey Heron (*Ardea cinerea*)

We saw you bird as you stood motionless.
Small stilted body, inclined head.
Until take off: when your arched span spread
into a sketch by Leonardo.
It's rumoured you've outflown the Lake,
become marauder, visitant, suburban
where that landing flap has not been heard.
And you pluck, plump, gold koi.
These koi, it's said, can differentiate
between their keepers and another human.
With teeth at the side of their gilled mouths,
they suck honeyed dummies, are chucked under chins.
Lying languid in their winter pool, you shock
and snatch them. Celebrant, delinquent.

TAKEN UP

ASCENSION THURSDAY Sandal Castle 7.00 a.m.

Not so different from first time
these disciples, making their way
with their preoccupations.
Heading into the breeze
they pass rain-soaked peonies,
lilac, laburnum and roses.

In pairs or singly they walk up the hill,
straggling a bit
on the steps to the summit.
Here they can see right over houses,
cranes on the skyline, ripening wheat.
The shadowed lake in uncertain weather.

They bring to mind this city of people:
those who praise and those who are seeking;
those already at work in this early morning;
those who lie dying or fearful; and those giving birth.
Those in prison, their hope almost drowning;
those full of joy, their happiness buoyant.

They ask for blessings aloud.
Pray for them in silence.
Sing farewell Alleluias.
Come down from the hilltop
to a morning Hope-charged,
God-dreamt, full of birds.

BLACKBERRY SUMMER

Along the lane
hooped hedges like curved walls.
A corridor of jet, black-beaded balls,
their filament spurs almost invisible,
goblin grapes, caviar, leaf-spread.

August
the worst in a hundred years, more rain
in a month than twelve, more rivers swollen,
light scant, rationed, the wind north-east,
the days, winter-cold.

Look at the spiders
their spun threads hammocking, rain-pearled.
I stand there solitary, eat my first fruit,
getting the taste of it, gather a greedy handful.
I ought to harvest, share fruity breakfasts

make jelly for crisp toast.   I won't.
Once a couple filled containers, intent, he
with a stick to summon, tame the brambles,
she, guiding their picking as it amassed.
They smiled.

My random, frequent feast continued,
raidings from this secret pantry.
I was Meg Merrilees, that inked illustration,
in a childhood book, as fruit left calyx
to my touch in juicy fistfuls.

Sometimes I'd lose one
to the ditch below, my hands hooked,
blood mixing, maroon and black, Rothko colours.
On those watery walks my hands stayed stained,
juice-veined, squid-fingered.

September   still the rain.
And still, surprisingly, the blackberries came.
The shadow scorch of summer, secreted
deep, in their black flesh.

VALLEY SUMMER

Every so often stone houses
lie on their backs
and laugh at the rain.
The valley has sky in its throat.

Lace in the hedgerow turns to spun sugar.
Moss in dry stone velvets new green.

Mill towns seam the blurred landscape.
Chapels and churches stretch needles to sky.

Then sun: woven air, bobbined blossoms.
Dog roses, lupins, slide from the sidings.

The valley is June-filled,
light-splashed again.

ON THE STOPPING TRAIN
for Northern Rail

When I left this morning you surprised me.
Formalities, affection caught my forehead
not my lips as I, hurrying for this train, was
already wondering where to hide the keys,
should you be out on my return.

But all day I'll probably remind myself
how that seemed important. That you got up
from breakfast, new brewed coffee,
came across the kitchen, held me.
What made you?

The dark imaginings I'm prone to
make me wonder if this is more significant
than usual. Is one of us not coming back?
Not re-entering that kitchen, not coming home
to warm familiarity?

~~~

Nothing original comes out of air.
Even the lupins by the track know that
and need to pay attention to the season's wind.
A railway carriage summons thought.

Inside this scarlet day, no breath of moving air.
It could be India, where Great Auntie Cissie lived.
And her four babies, all dead before they walked.
There's heat and flies and thud of bodies, heaving
through the door. The smell of chips.
A Northern train: doors shut. We're on our way.
Pennine countryside spreads to cooling towers,
and platforms hollowed out of hills.

Cissie went to the hills at Monsoon time; I wear
her golden bangles. Here a bearded passenger
has two caged birds. They squawk.
It sounds suspiciously like *God Save the Queen.*
He puts a green felt over them. A few rustles
and the birds are quiet. Reedy music starts.
A young man opposite hums behind dark glasses.
Outside, lupins give way to scarlet rhododendrons.

The connecting train has *L'Al Hari* written on the outside.
And I'm the only passenger who isn't young and Asian.
Unlike me, I'd guess they're Yorkshire born.
Each breath's an effort, eyelids droop, reality
is shimmering, gives way, to sand clouds,
flat-roofed dwellings, the trebling call of *muezzin.*
A water-seller on the platform pedals slowly.
Reaches for rupees, beakers he fills with a ladle.
And such deftness that he does not spill a drop.

~~~

Trains fill up. They gather in their passengers
like God on Judgement Day. That woman over there,
red top and face to match, wide open mouth.
Maybe she's died. Maybe that's how I'll die one day,
on a hot train, somewhere between Halifax and Agbrigg.
Life, but a journey as they say. Late afternoon, no shade
though the floor's a chequerboard of shadows.
Top windows, ruffian proof, as open as can be.
But still no air. The sky is glowering.

Squint, through dusty glass to passing fields of rape,
clusters of brick houses, a platform, cross-hatched
by fence. And passengers, who board this train.
At last thunder.
Rain is vanishing the hills.
All down the line memories go missing.
Graffitti looms, tags of giant palettes curve the wall.
Two high-rise blocks, called Poplar and New Grange.
No visible tree, no washing fluttering in the breeze.
No one calling children's names from balconies.

Bordering the track, pink and purple lupins.
A guard of honour, their stems to attention.
We slow. Then stop.
And here the hanging baskets overflow
with artificial flowers.
On a rain-soaked seat,
two lovers nibble ears, oblivious.

LATE

I dreamed of Taiaroa
and the sea cliffs outside Dunedin.
I dreamed of albatross.
And how we whispered
when we watched them, nesting.

I woke off balance, could still see
cotton grass dancing in the tussock
and white asphodel.
Snow grass, snow berries
beaded like unwelcome hail.

Then I saw you, clearly,
lying on your side, your bird limbs
drawn to your chin.
The whole of you poised for flight.
Your face, on that smooth pillow,

when I got there
it was already marble.

REMEDY *(for H)*

I felt like the envelope you sent.
Uneven contents, barely covered,
torn about the corners.
But I recognised your writing.
And your kindness
with its seal intact.

Bach's Flower Remedy:
Four drops in water to sip at intervals
Or four on the tongue.

Five dilutions of flower extract:
Rock Rose, Impatiens, Clematis,
Star of Bethlehem.
And Cherry Plum
in grape alcohol solution.

I looked up Bach in my C.O.D.
n. (colloquial, New Zealand)
a small hut by the seaside. There
by the roaring waves, I am measuring
your thoughtfulness.

The rose is spreading colour to the rocks.
The jewelled impatiens cascades over terra cotta.
Clematis trails its vanilla perfume
like your gesture, that star of Bethlehem,
that cherry plum, unexpected, friendship.

RED PEPPER TIME

Sometimes it's a shame to cut them,
snap the stalk, knife down the curve,
never the same on any one shape
of the red skins, shiny as patent.

I carve out the fibrous white and the seeds,
in excess you'd think for just the one fruit,
grown from its green, yellow, orange to red.
Capsicum, even the word like a blessing.

The oven is heating, humming less
than the home-going traffic. On the radio
Springsteen is singing, breathy at first, then belting
like that summer in Roundhay, his pin-man frame

on a stage miles away, outdoors smoke
and the music rolling, all of us
on the dark grass, dancing.
I take the blue dish, start carving, de-seeding again.

Small craft the peppers, moored close to each other.
I put in their cargo: chopped garlic first, peeled tomato.
Dull redness receives an oily anchovy, glistens
like the twilight's sheen, at evening's horizon.

CEREMONY

By Hardcastle Crags at Festival time,
a fallen tree trunk shone fluorescent blue.
A beech branch fluttered home-made flags.
A flock of papier-mâché crows
heard a wind chime played on copper pipes.
An angel beckoned through a half-open door.

We walk on stepping stones
a foot above the water.
Suddenly we're children,
leg stretching, weight shifting.
Late afternoon sun.

Upstream, a heron, stone it seems
until a head turn, an enquiring beak.
It starts to move, slow
as a major domo, a grand vizier
picking his way, one lifted leg
high after another.

But as we smile, sun streaking through trees,
each wing extends a span, almost too wide
for that short neck,
the small head, sunk into itself.

The heron flies.
We are mid-stream, motionless.

SUMMER LAKE FROM CASTLE RUIN

High up there you see what
survives — the violent sunlight.
And feel no particular sadness.
The lake below, red sails.

The wind in the bright heat
makes a sound like water.
You see the wind
in the whitening wheat.

Dog, poppies, dry beck bed.
The shouts of playing children.
Remember all of it.
There is such poetry in *gladness.*

CELEBRATION

The years are stretching, her yarn used and re-used.
Her cloth, more in tune with her weave.

She watches the young, spinning their newness.
Her love pattern spreads over table and feast.

Her shawl in the wind, when deep colour fades,
like the mat of a nomad, she'll roll up her life.

WINDFALL

Between the avenue of trees
lie scattered, sunlit apples. They wait
in ruffs of purple leaves, like fairy globes
or boules laid out for our selection.
We heard their thud.

We gather them; fill buckets, bowls and bags.
They smell of outside, blossom-time,
of smooth-cheeked sun and rain.
Then comes the peeling, slicing.
I remember Daisy, the way she pared,

her long unbroken strip of peel, layering
and circling the blue-rimmed plate.
Her thin-bladed knife, bone-handled.
I waited for that knife to make one slip, one
weakening of that magic coil I'd wish on.

So many apples: to give away, free garden gold.
We watch the big pan filled to the brim.
The steamy kitchen billows its pale foam,
cloves dancing as it bubbles, slices disappearing
into lemon softness. The tart taste
of another Autumn on the tongue.

YOU CANNOT BE A POET UNLESS YOU HAVE MET THE MOOSE ON THE ROAD AND WORKED OUT WHAT TO DO WITH IT (OR FOR MOOSE READ MUSE)

(for Sally, who is better than any Muse and partial to long titles)

Every so often you think you might be a poet.
Might have laid out the twigs of a verse
on the beaten track or the mountain path.
Or, on a very good day, a sonnet in the sunlight, even
under duresse, a villanelle in the cloistering evening.

But you know, that real poets always rise
from their car or train seats, or move down bus aisles,
where they have been thinking about nothing
or what they need for tea,
when, whatever they are travelling in, comes to a sharp halt.
And the headlights (because normally it is in the dark)
pick out that image, there, in a flash, indelible
for that moment. And they have to look at it, unmistakeable
against the blue-black sky.

It will be the Moose.
Either antlered, so that the huge head
seems to touch the tree tops.
Or, the creature will be swaying in late pregnancy
across the clearing.
Either way, there will always be a cliff top
or ravine to hand.
And, although there could be a score of other people
on that bus or train, or a fellow passenger in the car,
it is the poet, who needs to know, what to do
with the Moose, who is blocking the way
and has to be dealt with.

The poet ruminates, but quickly, because this is Moose time.
And people need to feel that, long after the poet has gone quiet
and the moose too, especially the Moose, there are still matters
about the handling and disposal
that require serious discussion, critical consideration.
And that is not nearly enough, it is only the start of it.
Not everyone will be in agreement
with what the poet has done
with the Moose.
As well as that, not everyone will like the poem.

WORDPATHS

When I met you that time, late afternoon
you said the day was *soporific.* I said, *Beatrix Potter.*
Then needed to explain how, at almost three I'd known
the meaning of that word, the way the Rabbit felt
from eating too much lettuce.

Walking on, I started thinking about early words.
How, 'misled' is a word I always mis-pronounced.
Still do, reading it, even soundlessly
with the stress on *mi,* like **thigh** or **sky.**
And even now, my wrong way seems to me
a fine degree more muddled, indeed more MISLED
(than the *'led'* part said as 'tread' or 'head')

Strange how meaning is embedded,
Peter Rabbit read as a night-time tale
for use as soporific.
How words springboard
in all our own directions.
And that's before some words or phrases
seem to contradict themselves

The day I write about, was one of *Indian Summer.*
And nothing like I'd guess, any day, in India.

ON DEEP STREET

A poem should be part of one's sense of life.

Wallace Stevens

ON DEEP STREET

Hesitant, they deal in a flare
            from the black-fretted lamp
on the shadowed verandah.

On filigreed ivory, layered
            dragons, dreams, characters
may all be revealed.

They might grab the sky
            fasten the wind to a string
stare out a tiger.

The dice stops, words
            are picked or plucked
to a pattern that suits.

They gather plum blossom.
            Scoop the sun from the sea.
Luck hovers over the door.

The Mah Jong players
            like makers of poems, place
their tropes on the table.

There is perfumed air
            as their fingers extend
moonstone and opal.

FIRST DAY

The words we need elude us.
Secrets, passwords, return tickets.
We wander through the bamboo garden.
Beneath the stillness of the lily pads
a family of turtles, paddling.

Memory is connected by forgetting.
On the marina we couldn't remember
the name for *geckoes*.
The ATM refuses your card. What
were we talking about? Planes perhaps
or Chinese New Year?

There's no escaping that red-gold, double-spread
in the *Straits Times* we saw, hours ago: here are
bargain trees in festive pots, teeming
with small oranges; cut-price pochettes
of gold gauze, zipped money for the Aunties.
The Year of the Ox.

The Ox stands for resilience
and bountiful harvest. Last year
at rice planting, in unusual cold
            (the worst, of course, for thirty years)
the water buffalo wore
their overcoats.

HIGH RISE

Breeze between concrete
leaking dreams,
the light trembles
in silver-skyed air.
On the dawn grass
will be miles of mercury.

Time's a collision
between light and breath.
Things crack and drift.
See how love can slice
like a singing wire
through time and sadness.

Night-lit leaves are still
under the moving moon.
Shadows pattern the path.
The air's full of footprints.

BAMBOO

Tell me about bamboo, its slender shoots, its silver leaves.
Bamboo flooring, fences, eco-friendly,
black bamboo and evergreen.

Don't mention pandas.

I've seen narrow-shouldered men shin up scaffolding
that from a distance looked like straw,
bamboo's brown markings caught in thin twine.
The higher climbed those hands
with heavy hods, the more bent the bamboo.

And I have held my breath.

Tell me about bamboo, its slender shoots, its silver leaves.
Bamboo flooring, fences, eco-friendly,
black bamboo and evergreen.

In the city centre in scorching sun
a certain climber seemed as if he'd pole vault.
Arc through the air, break his frail frame, crack
his head, wrapped in raggy, red bandana.

That day it happened.

RODIN HARVEST

Beyond the low wall of the guest house garden,
four heads move past in wide straw hats.
One has a table, another, shallow bowls,
another a scythe wrapped in a mat.
The heads turn, smile, stay erect.
There's chatter, musical in the early heat.
Four women and a swaddled child, close now
at the field edge, they arrange their tools.

One woman cuts the rice, gathers it.
Hands her sheaf to another, who threshes hard
against the table. The others stoop, to collect the grain.
What we thought hats, are now employed as sieves.
With these the women dance, arms stretched,
their bodies swaying graceful circles.
They move in unison until a closing bow,
to tip grain into the bowls. We sit, so idly,
too hot to do anything but breathe.
At midday, the harvesters file past again, more slowly.

TE ROA ARA
(Maori: the long path)

Along the spine of the headland
the hired car crawls.
The sign for falling rocks repeats, repeats.
Loose gravel jets from hissing tyres.

Brown mountains scowl.
Butt out of the sea, lie
like bull seals outcropping
their own ledges.

At a stopping place, an endless lake,
a wordless mouth, glassy basalt
a shiny-surfaced lid. But closer,
wind-waves whisper into edges.

The sky would make you think it midday
not suppertime
the sun's burn strong
on the fly-winged windscreen.

Behind, the long white cloud
is banked like dolphin between leaps.
Ahead, it's beaten egg-white, held
against a smooth bowl of blue.

At Punakaiki, there's fresh bread
brown eggs, black-gilled mushrooms.
            A bottle of Spy Valley red.

PINK SHIRTED

We'd come for the mangroves.
Come to see swamp birds. It was 36° C.
They wanted a man in a pink shirt.
So you posed with the team
while I clicked their camera.

There's something about an Australian voice
like a harbour with boats, like a wide open sky.

As well as you, there was the woman
with red hair, in pigtails, big smile,
bright yellow shorts and a very tight top.
Two thin, serious men, one with dark glasses.
And a third with the sweat running off him,
his girth, not easy to fit in the frame.

After the photo they smiled. We smiled.
The pavement was melting; air was elsewhere.

We'd come for the mangroves, the only swamp
of its kind in the heart of a city. Egret and ibis
picking about, ancient roots and the mud.
Then they read their instructions.
You wouldn't be...foreign? the woman said.
Then could you? Would you both pose for us?

But we need a newspaper, the big man said.
They have to be holding a newspaper.

As if on a runway, his voice lifts
at the end of the line to a cruising height.
So we posed, with our paper that told
which park had the jazz band playing.

We smiled. They smiled. *It was*
they said, *their Team Building Day.*
And thanked us profusely. Asked us back
to the pub for more talk, another cold beer.
On a boat, on a plane, to the wide open sky

as we edged away, to the mangroves.

IN THE FOREST

Between the boab trees
crouch the Yarrabah,
their tipped spears, balanced.
White and ochre markings
fluorescent against foliage.
So proud a people lie in shopping malls,
made dumb with so much liquor.
Empties, strewn and clanging.
At night, I hear their footfalls
and their shouting.
They are angry in the forest.

LAKE WAKATIPU

And on the lake,
sometimes quiescent like a windowpane, stippled water
behind which leafage and swollen twigs revolve.

At other times the waves snap, fierce enough
to whip at kayaks, take out tent poles. Today
the water's dark as legend
and as deep.

And in the forest,
an afterglow of resin, pine and eucalyptus.
And you imagine fridgefuls of rare homebrews
or spliced berry tots handed out to travellers.

One tree trunk is wrapped waist high around another.
The floor is padded with fresh cones
that smell — of jam, raspberry
at that point where the fruit froths

and a knob of butter's needed
to stop the red foam rippling over.
A bird calls; another answers.
Then, a chorus of sound sustains.

AUCKLAND CHOWDER *(for T)*

Remember that seafood chowder down at the harbour place,
a bowl so big it needed our two spoons clattering at the rim,
our tongues shocked at the heat of it?
Creamy saltiness, the floating prawns, scallops slipping
as we dipped them out with chunks of bread.
Remember those small cries we made, how we felt in tune
that day with every wheeling seagull. How sitting there
in that unlikely place, next to the Pacific,
we remembered other sea sides, other times.

That photo of you with your mum and dad
walking on the front at Weymouth, you're in the gabardine
that was to cause such heartache when you scorched it.
Your brother Mike is there, both of you city boys,
only at the seaside with your parents for that day
and free for a while from being Evacuees,
where the woman of that house had screeching fits
and never gave you jam on wartime bread.
Your dad's in his white shirt-sleeves and his specs.

Your mother's smiling, walking on that prom,
both of them much younger than we are now.
Then I remembered Cromer, Blakeney,
Wells-next-the-Sea, watercoloured into memory.
Postcard pine forests at the back of sand,
straw-hatted women in those striped deck chairs.
My grandmother, who swam until she couldn't walk.

And in the beach hut, there was her strawberry jam
on thin brown bread, and fresh shrimps she had
from boats down on the quay.

Yet this remembering is only snapshot.
There's a more recent world, a chowder of shared time.
Our children, and their children, writing the date
with spades on sandy beaches.
So many different seasides.
Such very different seas.

COLOUR TRAVELS

Agapanthus, blue and white.
The blue, that linen wedding coat,
Mandarin collar, silk toggle-fastened
slanting pockets, hand-embroidered.

It's the blue of Kaikoura sky
only feather clouds to frame it.
It is hyacinth, travelling light,
bluebell, a certain stroke-me pansy.

The white is that china bowl
the miso soup was served in,
a cloth of white, white linen
on the rickety bamboo table.

MARILYN AT ST. KILDA'S

In a café called *Monroe's* she's everywhere.
Arms up, hands down, blown baby hair.
Her wide gaze stares from all the walls.
And in that stepped-up Warhol way, one image
in the strapless dress, follows you upstairs.
Even in the Ladies, she is innocent
through articulate graffiti. Below, etched
in black and white, she's emerging
from a limousine in ermine, bewildered
on a subway train, rapt in Arthur Miller glasses.

Or in that hooded wrap, white towelling
and only thigh-high with the breakers foaming.
Behind a pillar near the bar, early Norma Jean,
ship's prow pose, she lies uncomfortably, open-mouthed.
Her signature now, a spider scrawl,
thick ink like icing on a cake. But black.

Outside, scorching sunlight and a grating
in the pavement. Young monroes (and there are many)
have sweet flesh like hers. But skirts too short to swirl,
in memory of that smiling Marilyn,
one leg turned inwards, high-heeled, peep-toed,
white-pleated billowing, frilled, out to the wind.

CITY OF SAILS

The moon makes ripples in the harbour room.
Blinds clack in the breeze.
In shoals of light, I catch that walk my mother
and her mother had, a kind of sailor sway
along the night deck.

The dead do not look down on us
from their glass-bottomed boats.
But every so often, voyage
in the hold of memory.
That unbidden walk

and a way of laughing, looking.
Ghosts own this night.
Look out there at the stilled waves.
Words anchor them. Stay adrift
as the moon floats silks at the masthead.

LOADED IN W.A.

Remember Woolworths…that emporium of childhood
penny presents, a foreign stamp or two, sweeties
from a row of big glass jars, portioned in a screw of paper?

This antipodean cousin has muscles bulging. Carnivores
stalk the aisles. Rows of red flesh, spread and cellophaned.
Racks of lamb, chops, steaks for barbies. Kangaroo joints
slapped against see-through plastic as if murdered at full leap.
Blood spatters corners of the pack.

Bags of flour here are outback size, eggs come
in two dozens and bacon slices stack in packs,
the shape of picture windows. Celery is stalked
small trees, asparagus is quatermass, some blanched
like early buds, some painted purple-tipped.

Shiny Sundowners, Fijis, Pink Ladies grin in descending rows.
Giant avocados jostle tomato globes, close to capsicums
yellow, orange, green; bushy broccoli, beach ball cabbages.
Produce of Australia in a store where supersize is normal,
serious over plenty, everyday.

We toy with purchases, as tourists do; tea bags, milk,
orange juice and water; unpack them in a borrowed kitchen.
And on the breakfast radio a voice announces: *Police*

are employing machine guns to ward off fishermen from
Indonesia, said to be setting up shacks, along the western
seashore, together with their cats, dogs. And their birds.

NOOSA AT FIG TREE POINT

Silence laps on the river of mirrors,
we see lace lizards, sharp-eyed koalas.
Think in travelling words, cross borders.
In dappled light, the boatman warns
Don't tread on tiger snakes. Time tilts.

And when we land, casuarinas, coolabahs
and those trunks that parent other plants.
Palms, their crinkled crescent leaves
cascade from cabbage pines. And always
eucalyptus in the air.

Bush-turkeys stroll, red-crested.
But mean-tailed, thin, unmagisterial.
Instead of gobbling though, they *coo*. As if
instead of being someone's dinner,
they have eaten well.
Among the ghost-gum branches.

EN ROUTE TO HANOI

We talk with dragon breath.
Eight hours rattling
and the bone-compressing bus
has proved unwilling.

Our two guides have ceased
their endless propaganda.
Stand as we do, watching
the back of a mechanic.

Across the road, in shallow water,
women stoop like wading birds.
A crescent shape of three.
One other, further, isolated.

Every so often
one of them unbends.
Then stoops again, to trail
the trap made from bamboo.

Against wide sky
the fisher women make a page of script.
This land's calligraphy.

UNDER THE FAN

Dresses move gently
    against white louvre doors.

A kind of picket fencing
    where ghost women walk.

Circular skirts sway, lift at the hem,
     kaleidoscope patterns,

blue-grey with white, bright blue-leafed
     against another's green.

Two white-gloved wives
    take tea in lawned surburbia.

A pair of gleaming girls
    skip to the college Prom.

In the glue heat outside
    the sky is tin

and a stroll away,
    untrodden jungle lies.

There, snakes still slide
    beneath the screeching monkeys.

As Sunday splits with thunder,
    the sudden slash

and riff of rain.

SUNSET AT ANGKOR WAT

Go dawn or dusk for sky behind Temple (Tourist leaflet, Cambodia)

Pressed against palm trees on the slope,
we try to be invisible, ethereal,
evaporate to the sweat-laden air.
Feet slip, skid; sparse soil, criss-crossed roots
have already sprung their snare.

Then the warning shout again   *Elephants.*

We grip the desiccated trees as a ruched trunk,
pink-ended, fleshy, not an ear away,
scythes the air with pneumatic waving.
Then, a cratered, marbly eye,
a grey sea of crusted hide.
Close mammoth limbs lift.
They take an age to pass.
Acres of sandpaper skin, slack, creased,
pleated over black moon toes.

We are prepared for the next one.
This time with a tattered howdah,
its occupants caricature colonial.
She in duck-egg blue, pith-helmet, pearls.
He, panamaed and looking down
to where we stand small, dust-covered.

And the sunset…? Yes. A fiery gong
that made a crowd fall silent, reverent.
The ground we walked was roseate.
And Angkor Wat? an imperial postcard of itself.
But it was the elephants
we took home with our luggage.
And, from time to time unpack
that lengthy lumbering, that swaying majesty.

AT ARLES

Crouched in the stubble,
there is no place
without giant-sized thistles,
their leaves and stalks
like artillery, like warning signs
that here is a place
where madness rules.

The sky has smudges of black, dried blood,
a sky that could shout any moment.
Clouds that could tip themselves, angrily
over your head.

The wheat husks are battered.
The seed pods of poppies
stand broken from stems.
Even the hedges are stunned.

There is no steeple, no roof,
no smoke wisping up on the sky line.
To the right, Vincent is holding
a dandelion clock, almost intact.
He leans back, blowing.
The flaps of his cap are well over his ears.

SEMANA SANTA *Almàssera Vella, Alicante*

Domingo de Ramos   Palm Sunday

The old olive press where I stay is alight with sun.
The Moorish fort is bright on the sky line.
In the citrus grove, we can pick all we want.
Taking only the fruit that is willing, that eases itself
into our hands, scenting our fingers.
Strange how blossom and fruit are present together.
These are good days.
Green shoots on the vine, the olives gathering weight.
A man with an instrument case walks past on the cobbles.
Then, the sound of an open air trumpet,
a drum and some cymbals.
In the square the village assembles; we form a procession.
We are led by the priest, a diminutive man from Rwanda.
All over the globe, palms are waving Hosannas.

Lunes Santo   Monday

When the sun is barely over the top of the hills.
When the Moorish fort is half-hidden in cloud.
When it takes till mid-morning to colour the pantiles.
The sky is dubious, not knowing how to proceed.
The swifts returning, swooping in on themselves.
A storm in the offing.
For all time, a woman breaks open
her precious possession. Her fine alabaster.
Now she is pouring the unguent
over His feet, massaging it in with her hands,
wiping excess with her hair.

Martes Santo   Tuesday

The storm hasn't arrived.
The heat needs to better itself, build up
pressure to a point of expulsion,
a no going back, a fait accompli.
The swifts are still here.
And the far away dog that barks all the time.
The shutters of houses are closed.
The wild white irises open their papery leaves.
Just two more days till He makes that cry.
Till He drinks from the sponge.
Till onlookers wonder if Elijah will come.
Till His Mother and John clasp each other in grief.

Miércoles Santo   Wednesday

When the curtains are pulled, there's no light on the Fort.
This is the day some call *Spy Wednesday.*
Over the mountain, the cloud looks like a length
of frayed rope.
On the Calvary walk at the foot of the hill
one purple iris, its dark petals staining the sand.
A clump of wild marguerites.
Gravel diggers work right through siesta.

Jueves Santo   Thursday

Dawn sky breaks to a grey. Against dark leaves
the oranges hang like small constellations.
Today should be golden.
The sun like a monstrance, transmitting heat
to a hardened, cold world.

This is the day of Love. He had come from God.
Would return.
But not before giving Himself.
They have been busy all day preparing the room.
He gets up from table, takes a towel
that's wrapped round his waist.
Pours water into the basin, starts
to wash their feet, each in turn.
Dust, dirt between toes, calloused soles.
Marks of their sandals streaking their skin.
Simon protests for us all.
If I do not ... says the Lord,
you have nothing in common with me.

Viernes Santo   Good Friday

The village seems dead.
All day the cats slink into shadow.
After supper we walk in the dark to the Church.
When the heavy door opens, light floods the Square.
Women carry out the bereaved Mother in black.
Her face, grimaced in grief, is almost a blur.
Four youths carry St John, who is dressed like a friar.
Then the priest in black vestments precedes a bier
with the life-size, blood-smeared body of Jesus.

The drums start up and the flute shivers in.
As we start the very slow steps away.
The villagers sing, the beat is slow.
The melody pierces, again and again.
Every so often everything stops
to ease round the narrow street corners.

Up and down in the cold night air
as the maze of the village unwinds.
There are tears, tears
as we file behind.

Near midnight we re-enter the house.
It's still, and unlit
as the minutes tick by
to *Sábado Santo*.

Today we leave. The luggage is stacked.
And two or three agree in a whisper,
they never found a funeral
quite so affecting.

And there were words within.
Words unheard, unspoken.

AS WELL AS SAINTS

Poetry is just the evidence of life.
If your life is burning well, poetry is just the ash.

Leonard Cohen

AS WELL AS SAINTS

As well as saints on the school walls
you had those droopy ladies,
two or three to a picture, in rich reds
and purples, clustered round a music stand.
They stroked a book or took their ease,
one idle hand raised above a head,
auburn hair flowing in their ringlets
or caught up in a pearl-beaded cap.

So many times you waited in long corridors,
came to know these ladies like your relatives.
Envied them their fur-lined, velvet cloaks; no one
ever turned them out to play in icy winds
or forced them to write letters home
that said, *I'm well and happy.*
There were scenes from Shakespeare too.
The fair Ophelia floated sadly on a wall,
waxen-faced, with flowers in her hair.

In classrooms you had maps and boards
for gold and silver stars and names,
inscribed for Special Commendation.
But best of all were the ladder charts, where
for half-a-crown, you could Save the Babies,
their cuddly shapes cut out and crayoned.
Then, as the thirty pennies were collected,
put him (or her) higher, higher up the chart
until you reached the rays of celestial light.
And white-bearded God, who sat in his long robes.
His arms extended.

DARNING

Every bit of clothing has a nametape,
the big blue knickers and the white ones.
I have a satchel, a zip-up writing case.
We have Latin, a *mantilla* and two prayerbooks.

I have a name, a surname, a box with sewing things
so that on Saturdays, I can darn the holes in socks
that Sister Margaret makes for me, by pulling
at the thin heel part so the strands give way.

And she says: *There: I knew we'd find you
something of your own to learn on.*
And so we darned.
The wooden mushroom underneath, stretching

the space our needles pricked across
to make the lines of wool, first down
and then the weaving, in and out,
which sometimes went quite well,

so Sister admired
the *handiwork,*
used it to show another hapless girl
how it was done.

These childhood lessons, so hard learned,
are folklore to my children, who
when their socks go holey,
throw them away. Like me.

PENMANSHIP

Today I found the bleached skull of a bird,
eye sockets in the small curved head,
long beak with two side indentations.
It lay alone like a giant pen nib, reminded me
of school and Penmanship.

We dipped in inkwells, set into the desk,
then eased out the pen, inspecting the stained nib
for fluff or sediment, that could bring huge blots
that smelled of iron and spoiled our *best* writing.
I remember the joy of it.

Up at the front, Miss Bowley making
marvellous b's, g's, o's and t's,
their straight and curly parts correct
and beautiful. We copied.
Fingers dented at the nib hold.

Once, there was a competition from the G.P.O.
a prize, half-a-crown that came by Postal Order.
The head mistress announced the win, at School Assembly
where we sat, fat-cheeked, cross-legged,
I was so pleased, I could hardly stand.

Up on the stage, she announced
it was *an honour for the school.* Sometimes
when asked to re-write an address
or people in shops query a signature, I think of then.
So much for Penmanship. Penmanship is no more.

The long beak opens, shrills a ghostly register.

PLAINSONG

It was stalactite frost that January,
the kind of creeping cold that chills.
At Christmas there'd been the dog,
promised as a present, never seen.
He'd been shot for eating chickens,
later they found he was not to blame.
The school trunk was packed, some Mars bars
in a Home & Colonial bag at the top right hand.
It lay under what was called a cartoon,
Leonardo da Vinci, Mother and Child.

Someone was very ill. My father told our neighbour.
His name was Bill.
  'Allo my duck, he'd say, even to grownups.
At Christmas the geese were plucked.
Bill would singe the last few feathers with a match.
He was the Beanstalk giant, hob-nailed boots
and a big brimmed hat he wore indoors.
He found a teddy bear once in the far field.
That year was going to have V.E. Day.
But no one knew that, then.

EPIPHANY

The gift travelled well. Sea-crossed and arrived
it was oblong, boxed but so battered *en route*
that the cardboard corners had flattened and broken.
And its brown paper shone with dark grease.

The goose smelled of country, lay with its limbs
tucked into its lardy white skin.
It was solid, shadowed in parts with sharp quills.
And ghosted in memories of strutting summer.

In the once-a-year oven, he'd honour the bird.
Carved the meat skilfully, drunk or once sober.
It was never fully consumed. At the Irish end:
did they think laughter, feast; there was not.

Very soon the poor goose would rest on the slab
in its gauze tabernacle, daily darker and dryer
down in that pantry, sadder surely
than any carcass around.

In Epiphany week he'd steal out in the dark.
Bury it, as he thought, far from the foxes.
In the moonlight it sat, big in the headlights.
A stray dog having the feast of a lifetime —
my father, another goose year in the Fens.

A RARE LIFE

In the kitchen, levering the lid of a storage jar
I replace it on the shelf and there you are:
taking a green carboy from the rack, light
on curved glass, labelled **TINCT.** or **MIST.**
And at your wrist, brass scales, dolls' house-proportioned,
for weighing out the powdered remedies
for flatulence, fevers or much worse.

I see you counting pills, well-trimmed nails, the speed
at which your fingers move over those spheres.
Or the two-coloured torpedoes, stamped *May & Baker.*
Your head is bent, your Humphrey Bogart forehead
parallel with the mahogany, I stand and watch
behind the reeded screen, where villagers can't see us.
You are a tall shape, blurring behind glass, measuring

millilitres, shaking a slim-necked bottle,
adhering the label printed with your name.
The local G.P. might come,
then you'd step out of the white coat,
fly those fens, talk yourselves
to Monaghan, where retting flax, mountains
and peat fires spelt home.

When I escaped from nuns, we shared that isolated house
along the River Nene. You had the Cinema on loan
from Fred, the film buff, who owed everyone some money.
We'd go four times a week; see every film that came
but hardly talk about it. We shared *a rare auld life*
as you would say. We shared of course a name,
the one that some time later, I gave away.

SLIPSTREAM

It filled up an attic
like a ship indoors
with masthead and rigging
of soft coloured wool: sea- blue,
brick-red, corn-yellow
and grass-hopper green.

The shuttle was arm-sized
for criss-crossing two sets of threads.
They moved like stiff dancing.

My Penelope mother had left her loom,
its threaded seas
and her half-done weaving.
She was gone for years.
Behind locked doors.

TELLING THE BEADS

First the Our Father, best of prayers,
stern, masculine. The Hail Mary's
followed, clustering, headscarved,

ten of them. To end, the Glory Be,
the white dove. That was the arrangement,
the pattern, a kind of heavenly tables

that at five, once learned, held fast
that air raid shelter
where we'd sit, blankets wrapped round

and hear the grown ups praying – Mysteries.
Even when we lay on lilos and flat pallets,
they would be at the chant, the drone

that held back doodle-bugs, Hitler,
prevented the place you knew becoming
photographs of rubble, skeleton buildings

with their eyes knocked out, their people
disappeared to smoke and atmosphere.
While we prayed on and on Joyful,

Sorrowful, Glorious.
And to the Son.
And to the Holy Ghost. Amen.

RIVER MUSIC

You kept it on the middle bookshelf
in that cold room by the river,
the rented house that recently
had been a hospital, our sitting-room
the Theatre, its ceiling scarred by lights.
An exile's place. Too many spaces.

It was a kind of ice-cream wafer,
the-not-so-gleaming steel of it
a bar code, honeycomb
with *HOHNER* written on the top.
You rarely played it, your life altered
by starched collars, pin stripes.

It breathed your other life, ceilidh
in the big barn, feet tapping
in the sawdust, the fiddlers
and your sisters dancing.
Often a neighbour singing.
You spoke of this if friends came round.

After a jar or two
you'd play your tunes, ending
I remember, not with *Danny Boy*
 but *Swanee River.*
The harmonica crying, sighing its return.

MRS. PHILLIPO

She's at the farmhouse door, giving me eggs,
a slab of butter and her smile. It's wartime.
Her dress encases her, and over it her wrap-round apron,
braided to her shape, wide floral patterns,
bright park flowerbeds
or the clock pavilion at Hunstanton.

Sometimes she'd say, *Step in my duck.*
And boots off, I'd see the dining room, its hanging
horse shoes, Toby jugs, the photo of her wedding.
Those huge chairs, red moquette
like the veined colour of her face.
Wide arm rests, seats, their cushions plumped
but lacking her bright-beam, dark-dancing eyes,
her quality of quivering.
I thought red jelly, lots of it.

And how are you my duck? She'd shout,
her back still turned. *Tha's been a long time away.*
I'll bet you've grown. Do you still like that school?
She never waited for an answer.
But wheeled round with warm buns on a plate.
I learned much later she was childless.

I'm smelling more than buns, or eggs and butter.
I'm smelling beaded skin, the sudsy, Monday copper,
other cooking, casseroles and slow-releasing juices.
On those collecting days, I longed for her
to hug me; her aproned body wrapping warmth
and me, tied tight, a swaddling
of her own loud leaves and roses.
Forget the eggs, forget black-market butter.

ALEHA HASHALOM

(i.m. Clare Chapman, Pennine Poet)

Had you been Egyptian, an ancient poet
and I your tomb painter, I would dab the hot wax
to show your strong face, bright eyes, blonde wispy bun
above rose cheeks, all framed
by those distinctive eyebrows; 'political'
I thought them at our first meeting.
But your art was not the politician's.
Instead of platitude, reticence spoke volumes.
And if you phoned, your breath-laboured voice
conveyed transparency of thought and trust
that made another's secrets bearable.

In the heart's dark where poems shelter, you
are fiercely here. Though it is already five years
since we said: *Aleha Hashalom.*

May she rest in peace

BLACKTHORN

Say the word *blackthorn* and it's Ireland, a stick
at the end of his loping arm.
Big boots, braces, string on the trousers.
There is lightness, language, that word *joy.*
But candles are guttering,
wax seals secrets.
Light, breath even are not for the taking.

Thorns, old scars
always the wounds.

Joy dances, is buoyant, bobbing
like heads over hills, Mass-going.
The men stay smoking outside.
There are too many of them.
Stories, the drink, childbirth,
fields and funerals, then the wake.
Peat fires, smoke in the square room.

There every summer, I rarely see green
but carved faces with voices.

They sewed lives together, left patterned spaces.
They sewed second-hand sacks.
They were God's armadillos, He
a hard father on nodding acquaintance.
Stalk to their leaves.
Dig deep. It's important.
The word *Blackthorn.*

MARRAM

In Norfolk that time, death
and marram grass tapped at your window.
You sat, an unconvincing replica,
one shoulder of your jacket lolling.
As if the weight too much
on your shrunk self, the tweed too rough
for such fragility. You wore a tie.

Outside, the black fen
was saying the unsayable,
marram and wind in the reeds,
saying, saying.

RIDDLE WITHOUT AN ANSWER
(for Thea, Jacob, Ollie, Matthew, Sophie and Hannah)

I am a patchwork of magnolia leaves.
I am the house martin in the eaves.
I am the helicoptering bee, the drum
and foam of a waterfall.
I am the snail pressed to the wall.
I am the ladybird who gathers all.
I am lopped branches, I am sharp rocks,
the cairn, the altar, the jack-in-a-box.
I am pebbles treasured from faraway seas.
I am the windows that nobody sees.

IN OUR HOUSE   *(for Hannah)*

At night in our house, clocks come off the walls
and dance mazurkas. Wooden spoons tap out a tango.
The fish slice somersaults. Shelves rattle, swop items,
mix up boxes. The fruit dish and the vegetables play tag.
Red peppers hide from oranges and grapes. Chocolate bars
nudge up to avocadoes. The freezer softens, opens its doors,
gives raspberries to the mice instead of poison.
The ancient cooker chats to the microwave.
Tells tales of meals long ago, the cakes that rose,
the jelly-belly Birthday parties.
A pineapple prickles to attention, rolls solemnly to the floor
and down the hall. Carpets stay put, do not approve
of nightly goings-on. But cannot stop the spiders,
who climb ladders of their own up to the ceiling,
pretending they are firemen.

SEEING WITH HER FINGERS *(for Thea)*

Two fat needles we select, like seaside rock.
Double-knitting wool, blood-red she chooses.
I cast on, scarf-width for her seven-year self.
Knit into the back of each made stitch
like her Great, Great Gran taught me,
making a strong edge, a kind of family patent
from who knows when.

My mother's mother knitted... swimsuits.
As you walked out of water, the pull of tidal current
made you feel your back was dragging concrete.
Her own one-piece she crocheted and lined with silk.
She swam, at Happisburgh until she couldn't walk.
Another Gran, the Flemish one, straightened her hair pins
and knitted yards of écru lace.

Thea's behind now, watching how the first row goes.
She tries a plain, one stitch perilously near the point end.
We recover it; start a purl, watch both needles dip
and straighten, red on pale wood, pale wood on red.
Until a row when needles move with confidence,
clearing elbows which till then, winged in the way.

She breathes out, as if the effort is more strenuous
than she first thought. She's saying softly,
Needle into the stitch, wool round the needle,
draw it towards me, make the stitch, And (with triumph)
slip it to the others. Her tongue-tip shows. Her chin
shadow boxes with her fingers. She joins the chain, the tide
of family knitters, her own pattern.

THE UNBEARABLE LIGHTNESS OF HANDBAGS

I carry with me all the usual clobber:
and an unposted letter, dog-eared article,
three pens (one leaked into the lining)
the photo of your firstborn, minutes old.

And there's a postcard of the Sculpture Park,
where when you came home that June,
we scattered my mother's bone dust, downwind
from a suddenly-arrived school party.

There never was such lightness
as those ashes.
I had tight hold of them until your whisper.
Then let them fall
beneath that light-filled, variegated holly.

GIFT *(for N)*

A hand came in the box with the new gloves.
And although unexpected she will keep it:

For it will colour sky at will.
For it will pluck stringed instruments.
For it will make those curlicues, no trouble, gold ribbon
on gift paper.
For it will draw and paint. And sometimes conduct.
For it will capture dreams that may otherwise escape.
For it will float, dance, when the other hands are busy.
For it will turn the pages of a heavy tome
or shine a torch in darkened places.
For it will scratch her back
at the place no one else can find.
For it will keep her hanging safely
while she's on crowded tube-trains.
For it will dust and vacuum
while she lies reading on the sofa.
For it will be so handy (oops) in the kitchen,
whisking egg whites at the same time clearing tables.
For it will stir smooth sauce
while the other two are chopping.
For it will find the secret chocolate and put it back again.
For it will wave, whenever comes the urge.
For it will be a gift.
And it came free with gloves.

THAT SUMMER'S END

Begging some bricks from a neighbour's skip,
he humped cement coaxing it with water.
While others shed soft tears he kept firm grip.
Trowelled his grief, laid out his daughter
and his love for her, not in the stiff linen of the time
nor in the ritual of so many deaths before.
But in his own lineaments, this tender lime.
He faced each day with wounds too raw,
felt her fingers in his calloused palms.
Heard her call, her cries, the bursts of her delight.
And if he dreamed, around his neck he felt her arms.
He laboured lighter when they'd met at night,
her head close to his, her face smiling, small.
That summer's end, when he rebuilt the wall.

THIS TIME

About this time of year I think of her, her birthday,
add up what age she would have been.
I do not do it sadly, yet.

Her month is full of bursts and buds, green everywhere.
Her name was Green, or became that
when her father anglicized.

Blue too, that chalky, icy blue that looks
so good near pewter skies. Skies, unending fenland skies.
I have her voice now, at its best.

Its over-optimistic best.
Not the other, no voice at all.
And I'm left to guess, antennae growing

almost quicker than my arms or legs.
Certainly waving more, picking up her every nuance
though of course, I didn't have these words then.

Words were not part of the exchange
and stopped altogether too many times.
Strange that later, not only was it words we shared

but colour-language, the blur and bleed of paint,
the deepest joy
that comes from darkest wells.

GREEN TUNE (*for Mabel*)

Think of green: new-leafed beech,
the striping in a snowdrop,
meadow-grass, un-trodden moss,
the heart of ox-eye daisy.

That's the colour of your jug
that one evening balanced
on your black piano. Not the top
but aslant, precariously, on the lid

that curves and covers notes.
Its colour sang to me.
I picked it up, went to place it
at a safer height, admired its colour.

Take it, you said. *Give it a home.*
It was in my father's family.
I felt pirate-like but took it
with me, at the evening's end.

Sunlight is on it now, on a table
underneath the hanging mandolin.
A pinpoint star is shining
on its no-nonsense curve.

What mealtimes, conversation,
trays or tables, fireside, garden.
Its handle makes a question mark,
nestles now near Peace-lily leaves.

MADAME BONNARD

Forgive me Madame
But what is your secret?
How do you keep your flesh so peachy?
Your limbs sweetly plump?

When he paints you,
Does he take up his memory
Along with his brushes?
See you standing, stepping, and lying so limpid
In that same bath, filled with youth?

When you crouch, you're a shimmer of dimples.
Your tender ablutions go on, forever.
Even your bathroom is brilliant,
Blue, green, coral, yellow, magenta.
You enter that bath like a stream or a fountain.
You never wrinkle.

Chère Madame, there are women
Who'd kill for your secret.

TO ELIZABETH JENNINGS

Hearing the wet tyres peel off the Oxford Road
I wonder where in the city you lived, exactly.
Where you walked, crossed the street and did your shopping.
I am staring at the house opposite, brick work
the colour of toast and I'm peeling fruit, cobwebbed
in strands of delicate white pith, sticky to the fingers.

The smell of satsuma fills the room; a jazz guitar
plays softly in the kitchen. The door, of that house,
is painted purple, a good colour in this soft light,
not brashly imperial, more the medieval mauve
you see in old Masters' or the Christmas card here
on my daughter's windowsill, sent late from Donegal.

I am wondering now, if on the house wall opposite
what I can see is stripped ivy or, something with a secret
that in Spring will come greenly alive, perfumed
and extravagantly deep-blossomed.

And I am wondering too
about these kind of days, when
even things I thought I was sure of,
suddenly sheer off steep, surprise cliffs.
Or swoop into dark hollows,
where love stops beckoning and hope
lacks the spur through faith's winter soil.

You never married, yet speak volumes of love.
Lexicons of tenderness, prayerful praise, lavished
delicately like lapis lazuli or gold leaf.
Some of your poems are illuminated manuscripts.

Yet you were deeply modest. And it's said,
dressed always in your customary woollen skirt,
hand-knitted sweater, hat and socks.
And even when you went off to the Palace
and met the monarch, who gave you an award,
you made only the one concession to dress
and bought new plimsolls.

I like that fine regard for unimportance.
And the shining confidence, when earlier you wrote:
The poem is a way of making love
Which all can share. Poets guide the lips, the hand.

ANOTHER BREATH

Poetry is when an emotion has found its thought
and the thought has found words.

Robert Frost

ANOTHER BREATH

The woman, swims by herself in slow motion
               past flying fish, feels their rough fins.
Seaweed is streaming her hair
her elbow crooks a nautilus shell.
                              She is almost submerged.

She has learned you can't tell a fish by its scales
that shells grow wise more quickly than people.

          There are rusted spikes, wrecks that loom.
Wood ribs that have held a galleon
cabined a merchant, a cargo of spices.
                    They still hold the bouquet of nutmeg.

Ahead is a sun-flooded schooner,
coins of the ocean lie in spilled heaps.

She rescues a goblet, its stem encrusted
               tiny creatures swarm out, wave thread tails
through sand-disturbed sleep.
                         Ragged claws scuttle their apricot way.
Sea horses rear, watch with globular eyes.
Anemones quiver a dance round her hips.

They fan out, passing each other
                                        over and over.

Still water is prism, holds the colour of crystal,
blue and yet bluer, bluebell with green.
                    Earth colours. She surfaces, slowly
to the soft wash of air.

IN PRAISE

*From a sequence of 5 poems, in response to the work
of Andy Goldsworthy at the Yorkshire Sculpture Park.*

In Praise

You are the poet woodsman, have kept
the fresh lens of childhood,
resisting the distracted gaze.

Escaped from clutching hands
who has not laid down in snow?
But you are proudly pressed
to a motherhood of earth,
our cellular re-patterning.

You teach us again to roly-poly.
To straddle walls.
To not be city sheep,
skating on slick stuff,
skimming surroundings.

You teach us
to be embraced by stone.
To stay near our shadow,
our moss-covered bones.

Stone Room

At the gallery's edge, the foyered oak
dancing its timber hornpipe.
It points our route to a room of domes, hives,
two burring the wall and melting through it.

Layers of rough stone, honey-coloured.
Pygmy huts, a hole for smoke to issue from.
Small steps, lipped shells, meringues,
Eskimo dwellings. Cairns.

The ancient art of layering, like lives.
The whole substantial, standing
only with each stone in place.
We start on the ground at crawling level.

Wood Room

Outdoors in: a coppiced cocoon.
  Curved logs, bark, peeling in jags
    in scars and seams, the knots of growth.

This warm, wood womb
  where chestnut twigs
    become capillary, pulsed life.

There's a stir, a hum, a creak.
  I stand alone.
    The dome above is a nest.

The ghosts of trees gather me
  to the bruise of sap and smoke
    to their raw smell.

  This flexed cavern curtails the light.
    But branches pattern an inner sky.
      Far off, there's a cry.

SOMETIMES

Sometimes she heard him whispering
caught the almost sound
a word
the trace of a bird on a branch.

Sometimes she heard him weeping
felt the almost sob
a tear
the trace of a fish on a pool.

Sometimes she heard him breathing
heard the almost air
a gasp
the trace of a man on a woman.

Sometimes she saw him watching
saw the almost look
a glance
the shine of his own reflection.

AFTER REMBRANDT

Yesterday, I kept seeing Rembrandt,
that self-portrait: gleam of breastplate,
proud-plumed helmet above the bleary eye,
the blebs, the lineaments of his courageous stare.

Remember too his studio, how empty armour
stood discarded round the place, north-lit,
overlooking the main street, one floor
above his double-cupboard bed.

I used to feel I'd welcome death. Now
I'm not sure; think of the silver slit of sea,
drained and dyked, the river banks,
my horizontal childhood land, the way
the rich, fen earth always met the sky.

Think too of something I read lately:
I must lie down where all the ladders start
Remembering that
and the steep sides of new-dug graves
how much, how much I'd miss.

Today, I touched a baby's toes, the unused
silkiness of scrunched-up parts.
Why is it, as we age and wear our skins,
the danger is we harden? To save hurts maybe?
The baby's newness makes a promise,
scarcely unfurled.

LAKES

Consider the depth of the lake behind the eyelid. (Irish Proverb)

We are, all of us, lakes, lapping over our edges
We are, all of us, lakes lapping over our
We are, all of us, lakes lapping over
We are, all of us, lakes lapping
We are, all of us, lakes
We are all of us
We are all of
We are all
We are

We are lakes

We are all
We are all of
We are all of us
We are, all of us, lakes
We are, all of us, lakes lapping
We are, all of us, lakes lapping over
We are, all of us, lakes lapping over our
We are, all of us, lakes, lapping over our edges

SLIPPAGE

After these weeks
lake has swallowed shore, slid
beyond its usual banks, its previous reaches.
Past reeds and roots, it dribbles tributaries,
little lakes, that hold drowned dandelions,
two beer-can submarines.
A willow, that last week curved on the slope,
drips leaky leaves
in the net of water.

Sky fills the lake all shades of grey,
moving like hammered silver.

A woman with no hair
sits straight-backed on a bench.
Somebody holds her hand. Both gaze
at swans, forced to a new perimeter,
far smudge of purple trees,
to closer greens, unstable, wavering.
Sun haloes a cloud edge.
Nearby, the warp and weft of gnats,
rain begins, again.

MEANWHILE

How lily-of-the-valley
with its spear leaves, flowers

even through tarmac.
How he, dressed in his old greens,

cuts new grass,
makes shine and shadow lines

across its breadth and length.
How this month marks

fifty years and still
she scarcely knows him.

How when April comes,
it still surprises.

FIVE STEPS TO A MOVE

Downsizing, that's what it's about.
  So why does every ceiling seem to touch the eyebrow,
  restrict the lungs, suffocate the chances of being *there*.
  And living.

This house, concealed, a drive more Bronte than an Austen.
  Or even Edgeworth with this frontage, jutting forehead.
  There are too few eyes and they are latticed,
  mean with the remaining light
  from Edgar Allan Poe shrubs, holly bushes.

Apartment. Fourth floor. Living like sandwiches,
  eyes at tree-top level, but no trees. Sound, even
  at a working time of day, like big dogs' tails, thumping.

Another semi, not suitable but reminiscent of the Odeon,
  loved and long gone, chrome-banded cement.
  A man comes from the Agent, slicked hair, like photos
  of James Cagney, that hung on staircase walls
  above the frayed red carpet, to tasselled curtains
  and the smoke-filled Balcony.

This householder, wider than the door she opens, gives
  warm welcome. The hall needs single file, a manoeuvre
  (or two or three) before it opens to a room,
  where the woman points to lit glass-cabinets,
  silver cups, all sizes, shapes, *For Running,* she says.
  Tells us all about it. Time stretches.
                                                    Downsizing.

HANG ON, MR. PRUFROCK

I have measured out my life with coffee spoons
(The Song of Albert. J. Prufrock) T.S. Eliot

It's not the spoons
but too much inherited linen, extra beds
except at Christmas and summer.

It's not the spoons but successions
of photographs, ageing in silver frames.
And too few places laid at the table.

Time is a breaker surging towards me.
High stepping, I try to resist the suck of the sand.
To keep balance, not drift, jelly-legged
to the sea bed, sooner.

I measure the walk on the high ridge,
the sound of the surfer's sail,
the new-planted cherry.

The painted interior, lit on the wall in sunset scarlet.
The gleam on the bronze, the dancing mote on the ceiling.
The ladder of light in the morning hall.

This is the measuring I do,
for dear life.

DARK

I reach for sky my father told me used to be blue.
Flare fitter to the Sun I am. Our forebears, kinsmen
to young Icarus, walked on long rays.
Now the sky's impenetrable, a pall of leaden dust.

Birds that may still be below, stopped singing.
For decades, only the ancients recall bright light,
tell tales of how they worked the fields,
fished wide rivers, glittering streams.

They'd shelter under trees, tassels of emerging leaves,
count damselflies at skimming play. It was prophesied.
 The sun is blown. The whole globe stumbles.
Landscape listens as shadow draws long breath.

I try to illuminate a darkened eyelid,
a shattered retina.

PENTECOST

(commissioned by Dean George Nairn-Briggs,
Wakefield Cathedral)

In the morning mist
And the breathing evening
You are the air
The flicker of candle flame
The Dove, in the eaves of the world.
You are the restless cooing
The ocean's stirring
The rounding of pearl in the ridged shell.

You are the heart's flute
The grain falling, the clear river
Running over our stones.
You are the summons
To other thresholds
To our lived and unlived selves.

Teach us to care and not care.
To be still.
The tongue of fire is wordless
The whisper, a mighty wind.
Anchor us, in the rise
And the falling away.
Hold us fast.

MINDSCAPE

Suppose they met again, on the span
of this steel bridge, the day pearly moist, sun faint.
What if they walked *splat* into each other?
Then as they side-stepped; he (never lost for a word)
would manage *Hello*. And a slow, *How are you?*

 She would probably burble of how she'd just had
a bar of the darkest chocolate. How the sweet-bitter taste
was still on her tongue… possibly, her face.
As if meeting him was an ordinary thing, here
far from her hometown, (and not his either.)
As if on that bridge, with its steel shining,
time dropped to the darkness below.

He might have glimpsed her before she saw him.
Seen her pass the four feet, the flimsy brown blanket,
the arrangement of boxes under the scaffolding.
Watched the young parents, playing with children
on the sculptural sofa, chairs made of false grass.

He'd have seen the trestles with wooden masks dangling,
all the cheap leather, embossed in fake gold.
They would have heard that thin man singing,
the other one drumming,   that same old tune.
Seen the sun on the river, the curve of the city.

DREAM

The dream had a tune: a man, on top of a roof,
playing a saxophone, loudly.
A woman put her ear to the window.
A boy smiled in his sleep and turned over.
A cat, hot on the night-trail, stilled its paws.
While a gardener hoped, that his cuttings had taken,
remembered the tune
and a girl from the war.
The notes flew over the chimneys.
Came to rest in the place where a girl sobbed.
And the sax sobbed.
And the sound grew sadder.
All through its fall, the girl wondered
who could be playing.
The man ended his song
with a soft *rallentando*.
As the dream
packed the melody back
in its silk-lined case.

GREASE PAINT

keeping
the whole show on the road
the tarpaulin trim
and the sawdust fresh
gets ever more
tedious.

there was a time
when burning ambition
lay in the wings
with the spangled costume
the starry tights.

but with lions to feed
and the elephant dancing
things got postponed.

the other acts zoomed.
the ring master swelled.
the big top flagged off
to foreign fields.

all shows
need an audience.
but applause is too thin
for the faltering acrobat
who trips on the wire
whose nerve plainly fails.

but who keeps on trying.

PAUSE FOR BREATH *(for M)*

Listen, I might say, time is short. Here's the map.
I'm at the end of training. The Docking Station's
Orbital, the Capsule, almost ready.

The course on Inter-Planetary Matters, I did o.k. in.
And that ten-day concentrated blast of Physics was a breeze.
Yes! I've done all the usual tasks. Been measured, weighed.

And know *exactly* how the toilet works.
The vertigo I've always suffered has been cured.
(Orange pekoe tea and lots of ginger biscuits. Try it.)

As for my fellow space cadets I love them.
Particularly the eighty-one year old, who has this sense of
Devilment, but is trusted utterly, with our Re-Entry.

Nervous? Was I ever?
This simply makes all the other stuff, well, earthbound.
Here, I might say, let's run upstairs and I'll show you.
All the uniform.

SHE BUYS NEW FRUIT

She liked the name, and said it out aloud, *Physalis.*
And tried to ignore its clear resemblance to a… *chrysalis.*
Wrapped in wafery skins they were, their flesh concealed.
And she desired their secret flavour when revealed.

She bought a box of the strange fruit to try at home.
(And knew he'd look them up in his great tome.)
She wondered if their flavour would be sweet?
What they'd eat them with, say cheese, or meat.

In their boxed rows, the physalis made a pattern.
Each membraned shape, a tiny Chinese lantern.
She always said it did you good to try new things.
These gave the glow that new experience brings.

They looked so *ancient,* as to defy all sell-by dates.
She couldn't wait to peel them, put them out on plates.

SHE LOOKED TO THE MOON

The moon shone so near
through the leafless trees,
she wanted a lullaby
or small talk of tides.

But the moon disobliged.

She tried sheep; couldn't do with their baaing.
Tried remembering addresses, recipes,
that one for *Smoked Pollock Chowder*.
The moon stayed aloof, rolling this way and that,
 beaming brighter through lace.

The clock too, shrieked its digits
and filched the hours of rest.
Her eyes were lighthouses, her lids
not so much gritty as sandblasted, powdered ash
from volcanic beaches.

A picture kept flickering,
Chinese children at red wooden desks,
their teacher out front at the blackboard,
their school, at the mouth of a cave.

The moon saw it all.

A KIND OF SILENCE

I have lost my map of sound,
my head, a conch in a rocky bay.

I miss the harmonies of talk,
the rhythm of dear voices.
Faces make dumb show.
There is no music but a tide of quiet.

Could this ever become welcome?
Could clarity emerge? My mind at rest
from a constant narrative, gathering
but needing less. At first a perilous bliss,

an unplaiting of the rope of words
to throw out to the darkness.
But like the shadow speech and music
in the stones of churches.

What if a gift is made? A silence accepted,
a settling to a greater presence.
A night sky of psalms, a goose's cello neck,
birds above their stilled notes.

Or will you see me with the wolves and gnats
at low tide on the empty shore?

ORANGE

In this heat colours stir.
Even the subtler shades whoop and chortle.
Colours can change though.

Who can think of orange in the old way?
Secrets in the toes of Christmas stockings,
sunsets, scallops, beach balls in the sky.

Now that you've seen
the shackled all-in-ones,
the bent figures, fettered, inching

in between the guards with rifles.
Behind the close-meshed wire.
Orange brings all kinds of anguish.

So much sadness hangs
like wet washing under trees.
Long ago, the hotel of dreams began to empty.

The ballroom barricaded. All windows barred.
Every staircase, a No Entry. In these times
when even colour is malevolent,

the heart, the mouth should stop
this way of happening.
Before the very air is in short supply.

WARRIORS *(for T)*

Fleece-over-pyjamas, you surprised me at the Station.
Brought an extra layer and my gloves, knowing
that the day before was weirdly summery.
Now sudden winter, a keen wind whipped.

In London streets, we'd worn no coats
yet holding up umbrellas in a November storm.

And how we sweltered in Museums.   I can see
those Warriors now, four abreast, larger than life-sized,
ranked for their First Emperor. Each one was different:
features, expression, even hats, buttons on the uniform.

The terra cotta was fine-marked, unlacquered.
Here was a kingdom buried: soldiers, carriages with horses,
birds, acrobats, musicians; their first colours gone,
han purple, orange, green, erased, like their young Emperor.

The clay remained; like lasting love
unvarnished, unadorned.

SURPRISED BY LIGHT

Coming late to slow beginnings, I like the leisure.
Love the way the new day dances
through the door's old glass.
Bless that glazier. I wonder if he ever thought
someone would thank him for his etching,
on their way to fill the morning kettle.

Everywhere there's light, it penetrates the place.
Fills the house like oxygen
until it swells with brightness.

A radio voice announces : *Lions at Longleat*
are to have their flu jab after all.
I make muesli, lay a tray. As if I am a visitor
as if like Morning, I am welcomed in.

Outside, light breeze, birdsong, fresh-gardened air.
And the patterned teapot from that market-stall in Asia,
unbelievably unbroken, all that long way home.

Porcelain mug, so thin the tongue
throws off the taste of toothpaste.
The blue jug for milk, a nectarine
and wicked, non-biotic yoghurt.
Then the walk through the lit hall again,
paintings deep in winter light.
Green ivy like a waterfall, sun
on the lemons in the copper bowl.

Josie Walsh was born in Cambridge but has lived in Wakefield most of her adult life. She taught in Comprehensive schools and Further Education at Wakefield College and H.M. Prison. Since retirement her poems have been published in a variety of anthologies and magazines.

A Pennine Poet since 1994, she is also a member of Wakefield's Black Horse poets and Treasurer of the Access poets. As a Wakefield Cathedral poet, she had two solo Cathedral readings/exhibitions: *Poems at Pugneys* (2001), *Speaking to the Mind's Eye (*2003*)* and with Access, *Journey and Place* (2005). Following an MA her successful *Breathing Space* was published in 2004 and a pamphlet *Here & There* in 2006. In 2007 she received a Diva award for Artistic Achievement and currently serves on the Diva Board.

Commended in competitions, Josie has shared her work at numerous venues and Festivals including Ilkley and recently in a series of Readings, to celebrate the 40th Anniversary of the Pennine Poets. In March 2008, she read at Adelaide Fringe Festival and had work requested for publication. One of her poems was set to music, another featured in 'Poems While You Wait' in Bexley Wing, St James's Hospital, Leeds. Sharing a WEA/Network Rail commission was appropriate; Josie writes often on trains, where no one asks her the whereabouts of socks or what is for tea, once or twice she has missed her destination...

She is editor of *Under Glass*, an outdoors poetry magazine at Pugneys Country Park. There, while walking, her own writing ideas or poems are sifted. Her work is nourished by reading, in particular Heaney, Duffy, Bishop and Eliot and by meeting other poets on a regular basis.
Another Breath is her second collection of poems.

ALL SALE PROCEEDS FROM THIS BOOK
WILL GO TO

Médicins Sans Frontières
was awarded the 1999 Nobel Peace Prize